the PET GET

RAT

ROB COLSON

WAYLAND

Published in paperback in 2017 by Wayland
Copyright © Hodder and Stoughton 2017

Wayland
An imprint of
Hachette Children's Group
Part of Hodder & Stoughton
Carmelite House
50 Victoria Embankment
London EC4Y 0DZ

All Rights Reserved.
Editor: Annabel Stones

Produced for Wayland by
Tall Tree Ltd
Consultant: Camilla de la Bédoyère

A cataloguing record for this title is
available at the British Library.

ISBN 978 0 7502 8929 0
Dewey number: 636.9'352-dc23
10 9 8 7 6 5 4 3 2 1
Printed in China

Wayland is a division of Hachette Children's
Group, an Hachette UK company
www.hachette.co.uk

The publisher would would like to thank the following for
their kind permission to reproduce their photographs:

Key: (t) top; (c) centre; (b) bottom; (l) left; (r) right
(Shutterstock.com unless stated otherwise)

Front cover: krechet; 1 Oleg Kozlov; 2 Eric Isselee;
4 (c) Roman Prokhorov; 5 (tr) Maslov Dmitry; (cl) Nigel
Cattlin/FLPA; 6 (c) Eric Isselee; 7 (t) Knorre; (b) USBFCO;
8 (b) Carolina K. Smith MD; (cr) Erni; 9 (b) David Evison;
10 (b) Eric Isselee; (c) robootb; 11 (c) Tafeya; (b) Eric Isselee;
12 (c), 13 (t) Maslov Dmitry; Evgeniya Uvarova; 14–15 (c)
Maslov Dmitry; 15 (t) Will & Deni McIntyre/Science Photo
Library; 16 (b) Polina Truver; (c) Ragnarock; 17 (t) Tony
Wear; (c) Shcherbakov Ilya; 18 (b) blickwinkel/Alamy; 18–19
(c) bango; 19 (t) Volodymyr Goinyk; 20 (b) Maslov Dmitry;
20–21 (tc) Anni Sommer/imagebroker/Corbis; 21 (t) Lana
Langlois; (b) Maslov Dmitry; 22 (b) 1stGallery; 23 (t) Joe Cox;
24 (b) Anna Hoychuk; 24–25 (c) fotoARts; 25 (br) D.
Kucharski K. Kucharska; 26 (c) Dignity/Dreamstime.com; 27
(t) Frances M. Roberts/Alamy; (c) Maslov Dmitry;
(b) Onishchenko Natalya; 28–29 (c) Africa
Studio; 29 (b) Michel Gunther/
Biosphoto/FLPA; 30 (l)Eric Isselee;
(cl) robootb; (cr) Tafeya;
(r) Onishchenko Natalya;
(b) Volodymyr Goinyk
Back cover: Eric Isselee

CONTENTS

WHY A RAT?

When some people see a rat, their first reaction is to jump onto a chair and scream 'Eeek!' But other people think rats make great pets. Rats are friendly, clever and fun to have around.

WHAT IS A RAT?

Rats belong to a group of **mammals** called **rodents**. Other rodents include rabbits, gerbils, hamsters, squirrels and beavers. Rodents have a pair of strong front teeth on their upper and lower jaws that keep growing throughout their lives. To keep these teeth short, rodents **gnaw** on things.

FAST AND CLEVER

Rats are fast, **agile** and great at climbing. They are also very intelligent and love to investigate new things. In the wild, rats use their intelligence to find food in unusual places. Your pet rats will need lots of toys and places to explore to keep them alert and healthy.

Give a rat a tube and it will soon be running through it. These young rats have found a spring to play inside.

Front teeth grind against each other to stay short.

THINK FIRST

Before you buy your rats, discuss your decision with your family. They may need to be persuaded that rats really are the lovely creatures you think they are. Also, think about how much time you will have to look after your rats, and whether you can give them the attention they need. You will have to set aside some time every day to feed your rats and play with them.

A healthy rat has four large front teeth. The bottom pair are about twice the length of the top pair.

THE RIGHT RAT

It is best to buy your rats from a rat **breeder**. You can find them through your local rat society. When you go to the breeder, take an adult who has experience of keeping pets.

A HEALTHY RAT

Your rats should have bright, clear eyes and soft, thick fur. Examine them for lumps or sores, and make sure all the rats in their cage are healthy. If one looks sick, it is likely that they will all have the same illness.

Baby rats are known as kittens. These kittens are still too young to leave their mother.

A GOOD AGE

Kittens need to stay with their mothers for at least four weeks. If they are taken away from their mothers too early, they will not grow up properly. Once they are six weeks old, they are ready to be separated. Make sure the rats have been handled from a very young age – this makes sure that they are used to humans.

BUCK OR DOE?

Male rats are called bucks, females are called does. Bucks are larger than does and a little less energetic. If you want quieter pets, choose bucks. However, bucks mark the places they go to with their urine (wee). We can't smell it, but other rats can. Some does also do this.

Bucks are larger and have fluffier coats than does.

Rats have good hearing – in the wild, it keeps them safe.

TWO'S COMPANY

It is best to keep two rats rather than just one. They will keep each other company when you are not there. Make sure you keep two males or two females – if you choose a male and a female, you'll soon have many more rats to look after, as they breed very quickly! The breeder will be able to pair up two rats that will live happily with one another. If you have the space, you can keep three or more. As far as the rats are concerned, the more the merrier.

Rats often fall asleep lying on top of one another.

RATS IN THE WILD

Wild rats have a bad reputation. In towns and cities, they often live in rubbish tips or sewers, surviving on anything they find. Wild rats can carry diseases, so it is very important that you should never try to take one in as a pet. Leave wild rats in the wild!

THE BLACK DEATH

In the Middle Ages, a mysterious disease called bubonic plague swept across Europe, killing one-third of the population. It became known as the Black Death. At the time, nobody knew what caused bubonic plague, but we now know that it was spread by fleas living in the fur of rats and other small rodents. The fleas were infected with a deadly **germ**.

Fleas spread diseases by biting people and animals.

Like wild rats, your pet rat will love exploring tubes.

STOWAWAYS

Nowadays, rats are found all over the world. In the past, they reached many new places by **stowing away** on ships. Rats breed very quickly, and if there is enough food for them to eat, a single pair of rats may turn into a horde of thousands in just a few months. In towns, wild rats are often thought of as **vermin** and may be killed to stop diseases from spreading.

Wild rats use their intelligence to find food almost anywhere. They run through sewage pipes and remember where the food is so that they can return to it.

IN FROM THE WILD

The rats we keep as pets are **descended** from wild rats, but they are much cleaner and healthier. They are bred in **captivity** and are not allowed to mix with wild rats, which would pass diseases on to them. Pet rats live longer lives than wild rats as they are much better cared for.

The Hindu temple of Karni Mata in India is home to thousands of wild rats. They are thought to be sacred, so nobody is allowed to harm them.

FANCY RATS

The rats we keep as pets are known as 'fancy rats'. They look very different from wild rats. Fancy rats can look quite different from each other, too, but they are looked after in the same way. Whichever rats you choose, they will have bundles of energy.

Hooded rats have white bodies and dark heads. Below is a chocolate hooded rat, with a red-eyed Russian topaz clambering over it.

MANY COLOURS

Fancy rats come in a variety of colours, from white to dark brown. Each colour has its own name. For instance, cream-coloured rats are called 'champagne', dark brown are called 'chocolate' and reddish-brown are called 'cinnamon'.

COATS

Bucks have a thicker, coarser coat than does. Most rats have straight hair, but a breed called 'rex' have curly hair. Even their whiskers are curly! Some special breeds of rat have no hair at all, but it is best not to keep these as pets – many rat lovers think that breeding rats without fur is wrong.

Dumbo rats are rats that have been specially bred to have big ears.

Dumbo rats' ears are big – like the ears of an elephant.

RAT BREEDING

Breeders try to make sure that the rats we keep as pets are happy to be kept by people. They choose friendly bucks and does to make their breeding pairs. The babies are very likely to be as friendly as their parents, and to enjoy being around us.

Rats are born blind and hairless. When they are small, their mums carry them around by holding them in their mouths.

MOVING IN

Rats do not like very hot or cold temperatures, and they must be kept indoors all the time. They need their own home to live in, which should be a metal cage with a solid plastic floor.

CHOOSING A CAGE

Pet shops sell cages specially designed for rats. Buy the biggest one you have room for. For a pair of rats, it should measure at least 60 x 40 x 40 centimetres. Make sure the bars on the cage are narrow enough to stop a rat from squeezing through and escaping. Cover the bottom of the cage with a **substrate** of wood shavings.

A SAFE SPOT

Rats can get ill if the temperature rises above 24ºC or drops below 7ºC, so place the cage in a sheltered area where they won't get too hot or cold. Make sure the cage is well out of reach of any other pets such as cats and dogs. If you put it on a shelf or table, your rats can watch you as you walk by. The more they see of you, the better.

Give the cage a good clean once a week. Change the substrate and bedding and wipe down all the surfaces.

Any small box can make a good place for a rat to sleep.

Purpose-built rat cages contain springs and ladders.

MAKING A BED

Give your rats material to make themselves a place to sleep. Paper towels work well. Let the rats tear the towels up themselves. You can give them a small cardboard box to sleep in, but remember that they will chew on the box and it will need replacing when it becomes too battered. Most of the time, your rats will snuggle together to sleep.

However tall their cage is, your rats will climb to the top.

PLAYTIME

Rats can use the bars on their cage like a climbing frame.

Your rats will need toys to play with. Many cages are fitted with ladders to climb, but you can add branches, shelves and tunnels to explore. However, be sure not to over-fill the cage as rats also need room to run around.

KEEP YOUR RATS SAFE

Rats will have fun with almost anything, but be sure that you do not give them objects that are small enough to swallow, and don't give them anything sharp. Do not give them exercise wheels, as they may injure themselves. Instead, let them get their exercise by spending time outside the cage.

AMAZING MAZE

A maze is a great way to see your rats' clever brains in action. They will soon work it out if there is food at the end as a reward, and they will remember the way the next time they are in the maze. You can make a maze for your rats using thick cardboard glued together with a non-toxic glue. Draw out the design of the maze before you start making it, and be sure to add lots of dead ends.

Wrong way! Rats have a lot of fun finding their way through mazes. They have very good memories, and will remember the way even days later.

Your rats will spend lots of time playing with each other. Young rats may also fight occasionally. This is normal – they are working out which one is the boss.

MAKE YOUR OWN TOYS

Pet shops sell plastic tunnels and slides, but you can also have fun making your own using cardboard tubes. If there is room in the cage, set up a series of toys as an obstacle course. Give your rats blocks of **untreated wood** – they will chew on the wood, which is good for their teeth.

DINNER TIME

Like us, rats are **omnivores**, which means that they will eat almost anything, including things that are bad for them! As their owner, you must make sure they have a healthy diet, so don't overdo the treats.

Rats love eating fruit such as watermelon, but they don't like citrus fruit such as oranges.

WELL WATERED

Rats need to drink lots of water, so make sure there is always a supply of fresh water available to them. Hang a bottle outside the cage and change the water every day.

When a rat licks the spout, the water bottle releases a few drops of water for it to drink.

EVERYDAY FOOD

You can buy specially prepared rat food from the pet shop. It contains a mix of grains and cereals. Rats also love nibbling on fresh fruit and vegetables. Try them out on apples, carrots and lettuce. Start with small amounts to see which ones they prefer. Feed your rats in the evening, and top their bowls up in the morning if necessary.

Sunflower seeds are a good source of vitamins but are high in fat. Too much fat is bad for your rat, so keep sunflower seeds as occasional treats.

TREATS AND EXTRAS

If you like eating something, the chances are that your rats will like it, too. They will eat sweet things such as biscuits and chocolate, but these are best avoided. Too much is bad for you, and will be worse for them. Give them cooked bones to chew on – the bones contain **minerals**, and chewing will keep their teeth healthy.

17

GREAT MATES

One of the best things about keeping rats is picking them up. Rats are **pack animals** and they will soon come to think of you as part of their pack. Eventually, they will love being handled by you, but you will need to give them time to get to know you first.

HANDLING YOUR RAT

To pick up a rat, put one hand under its chest, behind its front legs, and support the back legs with your other hand. Always hold a rat with both hands and be firm but gentle. Don't squeeze, and never pick a rat up by its tail – you will hurt and frighten it. Very soon, your rats will start to like being picked up.

Your rats should see you as their pack leader.

Use both hands to pick up your rat. If it struggles, put it down again immediately. You shouldn't force a rat to do anything it doesn't want to do.

Your rats will probably want to sit on your shoulder. When they do this, be sure not to make any sudden movements, or they may fall off.

A HAPPY RAT

Rats love being tickled around their necks. In fact, it makes them laugh! We can't hear rat laughter because it is very high-pitched, but other rats can. Happy rats make other sounds that we can hear. A contented rat may grind its teeth or make little 'chuckle' sounds.

Kittens love each other's company and often pile up on top of one another.

SETTLING IN

Remember that you will look like a giant to your rats, and they need to learn that you are not going to hurt them. Give them time on their own to explore their new home before you try to handle them. They may soon be demanding your attention, but if one of your rats is shy, give it time. You can coax it out by placing food at the front of the cage, but it may need some time to pluck up the courage to eat it.

OUT AND ABOUT

It is very important to take your rats out of their cage for about an hour every day to exercise and explore. If you do it at the same time each day, they will soon learn that it is playtime, and will be waiting to come out when you arrive.

STOP, THIEF!
Rats love collecting anything that is small enough for them to pick up. They'll even take your keys if they see them! Try to find out where your rats' secret hiding places are. You may find a missing item there.

A rat will find plenty to steal around a Christmas tree. Be careful there is nothing there that it can choke on.

CHEW ALERT!
When playing with your rats outside their cage, keep them in one room and watch them carefully. Otherwise they might get lost. Get down on all fours and have a look at the room from a rat's point of view. Look for gaps in walls and furniture – these will need to be covered up. Make sure all electric cables are covered up – rats can be killed by an **electric shock** if they chew through a cable.

RATS AND OTHER PETS

When you take your rats out of their cage, you must never leave them alone with other pets. Cats and dogs may kill rats if they get the chance, and rats themselves can kill or frighten smaller pets such as hamsters and gerbils.

GOING AWAY

Your rats are your responsibility and you must make sure that they are properly looked after when you go away. You will need a rat sitter who likes being around rats. Tell your sitter exactly how much food and water to give the rats, and if possible choose someone who will take them out and play with them.

Rats will climb anything. These have found their way onto a rope.

Is that another rat in there?

Your rats will investigate anything they find in the room. Watch how they react to different things. A mirror can be particularly puzzling for them.

HEALTH CHECK

Rats don't get sick very often, but when they do, it can be very serious. If you catch the illness early, there's a good chance that your rat will get better, so make it part of your daily routine to give your rats some basic health checks.

BODY CHECK

When you pick up your rats, make sure their coats are clean and soft, and their skin is smooth. Feel for any lumps. Rats sometimes develop firm bumps. These are usually harmless, but unfortunately, rats do sometimes develop **cancer**. If the lump keeps getting bigger, ask a vet to check it out.

STRANGE BEHAVIOUR

Rats are creatures of habit, which means that they like doing the same things each day. You will soon learn your rats' habits and recognize when they change. Any changes are likely to be the result of illness. Things to look out for:

- Loss of appetite.
- Is your rat less energetic than usual, or losing its balance when it climbs?
- Is its coat starting to look scruffy?
- Is the rat wheezing when it breathes?

A rat's nose should be slightly wet, but a runny nose that is very red is a sign that the rat may be getting sick. Rats sneeze sometimes even when they are healthy, but a rat that is sneezing all the time may be ill.

TOO HOT OR COLD
Rats are very sensitive to changes in temperature, especially when they are old.

- If your rats have been left next to a hot radiator for too long, they may overheat and start breathing very rapidly. If you notice this, move the cage to a cool place and give your rats some cool water to drink.

- If they are left in a very cold place, they could suffer from **hypothermia**. Their bodies will hunch up and they will not have any energy. The best way to warm them up is to hold them in your jumper next to your warm body. A drink of warm water or milk will also help. If a rat doesn't get better within a few minutes, you will need to take it to a vet.

Rats love hiding in your clothes. If a rat is cold, your body heat will help it to warm up.

POO WATCH
When you clean your rats' cage, check their droppings. They should be solid but soft, and long and rounded. If they are runny or hard, this is usually a sign of a problem with your rat's diet. Too much dried food can cause hard poo, while too much fruit can cause runny poo. Changing a rat's diet will often solve a poo problem.

AT THE VET

These are some of the more common health problems that mean it is time for a visit to the vet.

LONG TEETH

A rat's front teeth never stop growing. If they cannot wear them down by chewing, the teeth can grow too long. When this happens, your rat may struggle to eat and start to lose weight. The vet will clip the teeth back to a healthy length.

COUGHS AND SNEEZES

A cold is a much more serious infection for a rat than it is for a human. Look out for runny eyes and noses and sneezing. If the liquid in your rat's eyes turns pink, it may have an infection called conjunctivitis. If you think your rat has an infection, take it to the vet straight away.

EAR INFECTIONS

If your rat is holding its head to one side, it may have an ear **infection**. Your vet can treat the infection with ear drops, and it will normally clear up within a few days.

While your rat is out and about, be sure that you know where it is at all times. Rats can be seriously injured if a human treads or sits on them by accident.

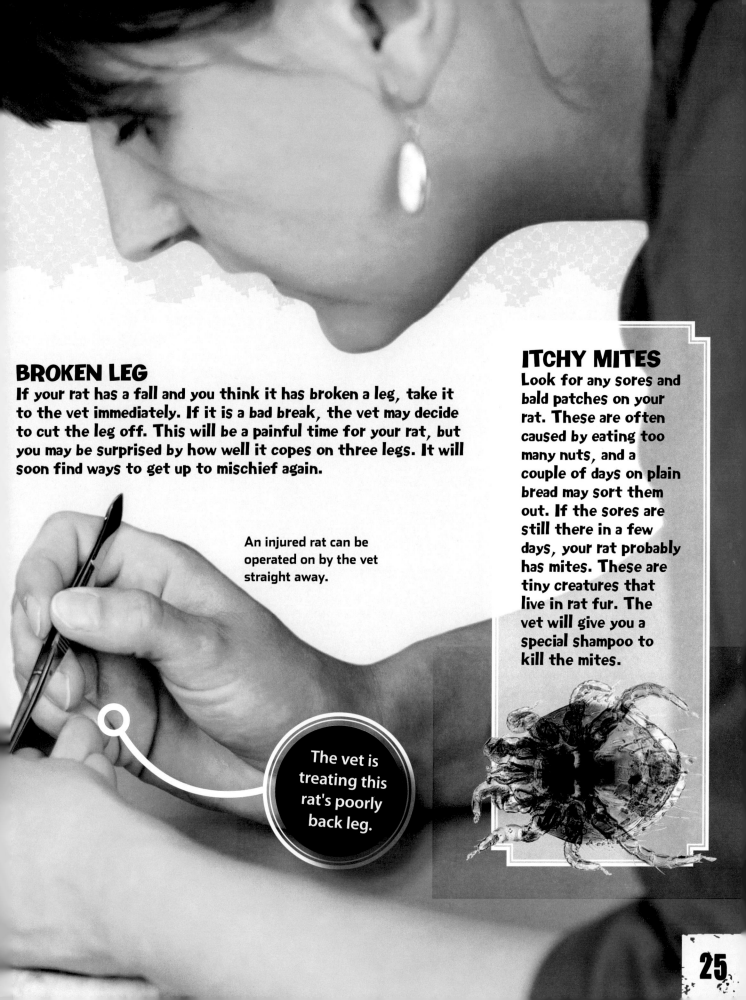

BROKEN LEG

If your rat has a fall and you think it has broken a leg, take it to the vet immediately. If it is a bad break, the vet may decide to cut the leg off. This will be a painful time for your rat, but you may be surprised by how well it copes on three legs. It will soon find ways to get up to mischief again.

An injured rat can be operated on by the vet straight away.

The vet is treating this rat's poorly back leg.

ITCHY MITES

Look for any sores and bald patches on your rat. These are often caused by eating too many nuts, and a couple of days on plain bread may sort them out. If the sores are still there in a few days, your rat probably has mites. These are tiny creatures that live in rat fur. The vet will give you a special shampoo to kill the mites.

RAT SHOWS

A rat show is a great place to meet other rat lovers, show off your rats and learn more about how to keep them. If you're showing a rat, you'll need to buy a special show tank to display it in.

LOOKING THEIR BEST

Rats are naturally very clean animals that spend a lot of time washing themselves, so some owners never bathe them. But before a show, a bath will make your rats look their best. Use a gentle pet shampoo and wash them in a bowl of warm water. Rinse them and dry them with a towel. Your rats may not like being washed, so be gentle.

Dry your rat with a towel after its bath. It may then want to run around to warm up.

A DAY AT THE SHOW

Before a show begins, all the rats are lined up in their tanks so that everyone can look at them. The judges take each rat out of its tank and handle it. They put coloured stickers on the tanks of the rats they think are best. At the end of the day, an overall 'Best in Show' winner is chosen.

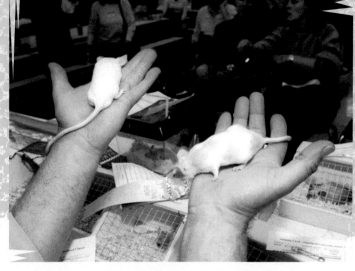

Rat shows are relaxed occasions – while everyone wants to win, meeting other rat lovers and their cool rats is the best part.

This rat may not look special, but it is healthy and alert, so could do well in the general pet class.

WHAT MAKES A WINNING RAT?

Don't worry if you don't think your rat is special enough to win a show. Competitions have different **classes**, and you can enter a general pet class. You may find out that your rat is more special than you thought, and belongs to a particular class of fancy rat. If so, you can enter it in that class next time. The winning animals are healthy, friendly rats that are the right shape and colour for their class.

This rat is a Russian silver. It can be entered into a special class for silver rats.

GROWING OLD

Rats have short lives and when your rats reach about two years old, they will start to become less active. One of the hardest things about owning rats is knowing that they will only be with you for a maximum of three years. You will need to take special care of your old rats.

A QUIET LIFE

As your rats age, you will notice that their bodies become less firm. This means that their muscles are not as strong as they used to be. When this happens, they start to find it difficult to climb, and you will need to take the ladders out of their cages. Older rats spend much more time sleeping, so make sure their food and water are within easy reach of their beds.

KEEPING A RECORD

Keeping a scrapbook or a website page is a great way to remember your rat. Include photos and any prizes your rat might have won at shows. It will remind you of the good times you had with your rat and the happy life it led.

CHANGING DIET

Old rats often have poor teeth, which makes it difficult for them to chew. They may no longer be able to eat hard food such as nuts. When this happens, you need to give the rats soft food that contains lots of energy. You can buy special high-energy food from pet shops or vets, or you can try them on sugar-coated breakfast cereals.

SAYING GOODBYE

Your old rat may die peacefully in its sleep or it may become very ill. If it is in a lot of pain, you will have to make the hard decision to have your pet **put down.** Your rat will fall asleep and not be in pain any more. It's natural to feel sad when you lose your pet, but eventually your pain will pass and you will be left with lots of happy memories.

AMAZING RAT FACTS

Rats are strong swimmers. They can swim for nearly a kilometre and hold their breath for up 30 seconds underwater.

There may be as many as 10 million wild rats in New York City. That's one rat for every human.

A rat's front teeth are harder than steel and can chew through wood, plastic and even glass.

The oldest pet rat ever recorded lived to the age of seven.

The huge Gambian pouched rat (right) can grow up to 1 metre long, including its tail.

When one of your rats dies, you may be left with one rat on its own. If you can, try to get it some new rat companions. Ideally, introduce it to two young new cage mates of the same sex.

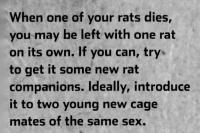

RAT QUIZ

Test your rat knowledge with this short quiz.

Can you name these different fancy rats?

1.   **2.**   **3.**   **4.**

5. **What is the name for fancy rats with curly hair?**

6. **What is the name of the deadly disease carried by rats that killed millions in the Middle Ages?**

7. **What is the name for a female rat?**

8. **What are baby rats called?**

9. **Why is it important to give a rat something to chew?**

10. **If a rat is not holding its head straight, what is the likely cause?**

GLOSSARY

AGILE
Able to move around quickly and easily.

BREEDER
A person who keeps animals to produce and sell the young.

CANCER
A serious disease that animals can suffer from. Cancer causes parts of the body to grow too much, and kills an animal if it is not treated.

CAPTIVITY
Being kept in a controlled space. Rats in captivity behave differently from wild rats and tend to be healthier.

CLASSES
The different groups of fancy rat. Rats fall into different classes according to their colour, the texture of their fur, their size and the shape of their bodies.

DESCENDED
Bred from particular ancestors. Fancy rats are descended from wild rats that were caught and bred.

ELECTRIC SHOCK
A dangerous current of electricity that can pass through a body when it touches an electric cable.

GERM
A tiny life form that is too small to see with the naked eye, and causes diseases when it passes into bodies.

GNAW
To chew continuously for long periods at a time. Rodents need to gnaw on things to keep their teeth short.

HYPOTHERMIA
A potentially serious medical condition that occurs when the body temperature falls after being exposed to extreme cold. Rats are very sensitive to the cold and can suffer from hypothermia.

INFECTION
An illness, such as a cold, caused by invisible germs.

MAMMAL
A warm-blooded animal with fur or hair on its body that feeds its young milk.

MINERALS
Chemical substances contained in food that the body needs in small quantities so that it can stay healthy. Rats need the mineral calcium to keep their bones strong and healthy.

OMNIVORE
An animal that eats both meat and plants.

PACK ANIMALS
Animals that live in groups called packs in the wild. Some of the animals in the pack are leaders, while others are followers. Wild rats live in packs of 30–40 animals.

PUT DOWN
To end the life of a sick animal with an injection that puts it to sleep so that it then dies. A vet will put down a very sick rat to end its suffering.

RODENT
A type of mammal that has four large front teeth that keep growing throughout its life, and that the animal must keep short by gnawing. There are more than 2,000 different kinds, or species, of rodent.

STOW AWAY
To hide on a ship and travel on it without the crew knowing you are there. Rats have travelled around the world by stowing away on ships.

SUBSTRATE
Loose material such as wood shavings that is placed at the bottom of a rat's cage. The substrate should be changed regularly.

UNTREATED WOOD
Wood that has not been painted or varnished. The chemicals used to treat wood can be harmful to rats.

VERMIN
Animals such as wild rats that are thought of as pests because they carry diseases or cause damage.

USEFUL WEBSITES

www.nfrs.org
Website of the National Fancy Rat Society. You will find lots of further information on caring for rats and details of your local rat show.

www.fancyratsforum.co.uk
Website and forum for rat-lovers. A great place to chat to fellow rat enthusiasts and ask any questions you need answering about keeping rats.

INDEX